THE ORDAINED SMILE OF SAINT SADIE MAY JENKINS

Reginald Edmund

BROADWAY PLAY PUBLISHING INC
New York
www.broadwayplaypub.com
info@broadwayplaypub.com

First edition: May 2024
I S B N: 978-0-88145-918-0

Book design: Marie Donovan
Page make-up: Adobe InDesign
Typeface: Palatino

The City of the Bayou Collection is a series of nine plays. They are the playwright's attempt at making a contemporary House of Atreus through a Afro-Surrealist lens. The plays, in order, are:

THE DAUGHTERS OF THE MOON

SOUTHBRIDGE

IN THE PROPHET'S HOUSE

BLOOD ON THE BAYOU

REDEMPTION OF ALLAH BLACK

JUNETEENTH STREET

THE ORDAINED SMILE OF SAINT SADIE MAY JENKINS

THE LAST CADILLAC

ALL THE DYING VOICES

CHARACTERS & SETTING

Sadie May Jenkins, *late 60s black woman*
Clarence Jenkins, *late 20s, black man, old school*
Ro, *15, black woman-child*
Smiles, *a smiling man, black man*

The burned out ruins of a small shotgun house in the 4th Ward of Houston. A pile of rags sits in the center of the house, there is a broken window to one side of the room and a doorway that leads to a porch outside.

Generic dictionary's definition of a saint: An exceptionally virtuous person.

Reginald Edmund's definition of a saint: A mother.

Dedicated to: Grandma Harrison, Grandma Bell, and all the women who raised me.

Prologue

(Darkness on stage, a woman's [SADIE] voice calls out.)

SADIE: God. Can you hear me? I need you...I need you to help direct me. Take away this pain, cause I want to die sometimes. I feel like this house, Lord... These walls charred and crumbling, my skin. These beams, my bones. I am this house, Lord. I feel it. It feels like my foundation is gone and I'm going to collapse on myself any moment now, Lord. I'm not sure what to do... This house ain't a home no more and I just want to smile again. Help me find my smile again. Just guide me, Lord...I'm alone.

(The sound of a bell, rings out once...twice...three times.)

(End scene)

ACT ONE
The Lost Girls

Scene 1:
Stranger in a Strange Land

(Tiny streams of afternoon sunlight cut the dark gloom of a charred shotgun house.)

(Soot covers the walls. The sound of singing breaks the silence. SADIE *stands by a shattered window; she is a beautiful elderly woman dressed in black which appears to have been neglected in its care. She wearily grips a bucket and rags. She stoops down and rubs at the dark soot that covers the wall. Each scrub to the wall that wipes away soot reveals a word of graffiti. She sings sorrowfully as if in mourning.)*

SADIE: *(Sings)*
Hey there compass, bring me home…
Hey there compass, I'm all alone…
Once was lost…now I'm found…
Once was chained up like a slave head bowed,
But now I'm heaven bound.
Hey compass, hey there compass…
Bring me home.
(She stops scrubbing and wanders through the ruins, digging, sorting boxes.)

(A bell rings once, twice, three times.)

CLARENCE: Sadie...Sadie come home... Come home to me...

(SADIE *looks and sees a shadowy figure standing in the corner of the room who begins to take shape in the darkness.*)

SADIE: Lord save me.

(She begins gasping for breathe and reaches into her purse and pulls out a box of pills. She takes one.)

(A girl [RO] runs into the house. She looks around and closes the door behind her. She finds a slab of broken and charred wood and jams it against the door to lock it. SADIE *looks once again towards the shadowy figure. Its' gone. She looks once again towards the girl.)*

RO: Help me!

SADIE: I don't know who you are, or what you want, but you better get going? You hear me?

(The girl is no older than fifteen year old. She's been hardened by the streets. She wears a baseball cap, and doo-rag, and tattered basketball jersey with the number 7. Her name is RO. *She sets a back- pack on the floor.)*

RO: I'm in trouble.

SADIE: What type of trouble are you in?

RO: Can you help me please? Just let me hide out here for a little while. Just for a little while. That's all I'm asking.

(She pulls out a cigarette and begins smoking it.)

SADIE: Did somebody else come in here with you?

RO: No...no...just me?

SADIE: You sure?

RO: Yeah.

SADIE: Positive about that?

RO: Yeah. Why?

SADIE: Oh no reason… Could you put that out?

RO: Sorry.

(She drops the cigarette on the ground and stomps it out.

SADIE: Listen, child, I can't help you, I don't even know who you are.

RO: My name is Ro…Ro La Branch; there's a man after me!
Some man has been following me, all day.

SADIE: Well, calm down now, why would anyone chase after a little girl like you for?

RO: I don't know…I'm scared.

Sadie moves to the door and looks out.

SADIE: Where he at?

RO: He's out there.

SADIE: I don't see nobody… You sure he was following you?

RO: Why would I make something up like that?

SADIE: Calm down…tell me what happened.

RO: He was following me! He was following me, I started walkin'… He started walkin'…I walked down the street past the convenience store, and turned the corner, and that's when I saw him standing on the opposite side of the street.
All I remember is that he was smiling. I started walking and he'd walk. If I'd stop, he'd stop. I walked through an alleyway and neared a doorway, ducked in here and that's when I saw you.

SADIE: What he look like?

RO: Strange—

SADIE: Strange?

RO: Hell yeah, he was strange!

SADIE: Watch your language... Now what do you mean by strange?

RO: He must have been seven...eight...no thirteen feet tall. Had rows and rows of teeth... Scariest man I've ever seen in my life.

SADIE: Girl, that don't answer my question.

RO: I don't know—

SADIE: Didn't you see his face?

RO: All I could see was a row of teeth. Can you help me please?—

SADIE: I got my own troubles—

RO: What if it was you who was calling for help? Wouldn't you want someone to help you?—

SADIE: Little girl—

RO: Please, I'm beggin' you.—

SADIE: No...no way...uh-uh...absolutely not—

RO: Please...I'm scared. I don't know what to do...I'm alone—

SADIE: What did you say?

RO: I'm alone. Can you help me please...I just need a place to stay till that man leaves? Just till he leaves... An hour and then you'll never see me again...I promise. Please? Please?

(SADIE *pauses and sighs.*)

SADIE: You can stay... No man is coming into this house. Let's barricade up the doors, we'll figure out where to go from there. You'll be alright. I promise you that.

RO: Thank you, thank you, thank you... Lady, I could hug you.

(SADIE *holds out her hand and stops* RO.)

SADIE: We're going to go ahead and skip the huggin' darling.

(The writing upon the walls glows, pulsates for just a moment and fades out.)

(End scene)

Scene 2:
What's your story?

(A little later, afternoon. The house's entry is blockaded by rubbish and left over planks. SADIE sits on a pile of rags in the corner of the room. She unwraps a half eaten old sandwich and eats. She offers it to RO, who is shuffling nervously from the door and back.)

SADIE: Hungry?

RO: No…no thanks, I'm cool.
(Pause)
I don't know how can you eat at a time like this?

SADIE: Well that's simple, I don't got nobody chasing after me, that's how. You make sure the back way is sealed up tight?

RO: Yeah…
(Pause)
What's your name anyway lady?

SADIE: I'm Miss Jenkins.

RO: So do we have a plan?

SADIE: Plan?
(Pause)
Hiding out here not a plan?

RO: Well, we can't just sit here and wait for the man to leave.

SADIE: Watch me, Child, watch me.

(RO *wanders around the house looking at the charred reminders of a life forgotten, looking toward* SADIE *occasionally.)*

(RO *examines the room, studying the place, every fallen timber, every shattered window, the graffitied walls, covered with soot.)*

RO: What happened here?

SADIE: I'm going to give you some advice. The less questions you ask, the more I'll like you. Remember that.

(RO *sighs, wanders to the window and looks out.)*

(*She checks her watch and looks out again, then sighs in frustration and returns.)*

RO: That man still out there. Been standing there since this afternoon. Just looking over here at the house and smiling. I'd wish he'd go away.

SADIE: Sit still for a minute, youth nowadays, I swear. When I was your age, I was never all over the place like you.

(RO *sits, and then as quickly as she sits, she gets up and sighs.* SADIE *and* RO *cross their arms at the same time.* RO *looks at* SADIE, SADIE *looks at* RO. *They uncross their arms. And* RO *rises back to her feet and looks out the porch door.)*

(*After a moment,* SADIE *rises from where she was seated and moves out to the window. She looks out, sees nothing.)*

SADIE: I'm not seeing anyone.

(RO *moves to join her. She looks as well.)*

RO: He was there just a minute ago.

(*Silence*)

SADIE: I think he's gone, I can't see anything.

Sadie moves to the exit and motions for her to leave.

RO: Can't I—?

SADIE: What? Stay a bit longer—?

RO: Just for a little bit? Please? I promise I won't be a nuisance—

SADIE: Child, I got news for you, baby, you already is. Look around you…it's plain to see that this ain't no place for no child.

RO: There he is! You don't see him? There across the street.

SADIE: Child, there's nobody…

(SADIE *turns and looks out across the street again. She sees a man standing the distance shrouded in shadows. He smiles and waves.*)

SADIE: There…
(*Pause*)
What's he doing?

RO: I don't know…I…I think, he's… He's standing there… Waving and smiling… He's looking at me… he's looking right at me?

SADIE: Oh what trouble did you bring my way, child?
(*She begins gasping for breathe.*)
This is what we're gonna do… We're going to hold out here for fifteen, twenty minutes, and he'll either tire out or someone might wander by.

RO: I haven't seen anybody since I got here.

Just don't throw me out there with that man.

(SADIE *takes her pill and returns to her seat.*)

SADIE: I'm not gonna let no man into this house. Just give me some time to gather my thoughts.
(*She takes a deep breath.*)
(*She enjoys the silence and attempts to return to cleaning the soot on the walls. Revealing more words*)

(She enters into a sort of ritual as her hands grasp the rag, plunge itself into the bucket and scrub at the wall. For a while this goes on.)

(Sings)

Hey there compass, bring me home…

Hey there compass, I'm all alone…

Once was lost…now I'm found…

(With nothing but the sound of scrubbing and her breathing filling the room. It almost soothes her. It doesn't last.)

(She notices something and studies RO.*)*

Do I know you?

RO: Nah, I don't think so…

(Pause)

So are you going to tell me what the hell happened here?

SADIE: Watch your language… It was…it is my house.

RO: Damn.

SADIE: I said watch your language.

RO: Sorry.

(Pause)

*(*RO *grabs the pills and looks at them while* SADIE *scrubs.)*

RO: So what happened here?

SADIE: Don't be stupid girl, what do you think?

(Pause)

RO: What's your story anyway, lady?

SADIE: Just because I said you can stay here, doesn't mean that I want you to talk. I don't want to know you from my own shadow.

(Pause)

RO: What the hell are you doing?

SADIE: Just be quiet I'm trying to clean.

RO: At a moment like this?

SADIE: When I clean, I think.

RO: You're a weird lady.

(Silence…)

(SADIE begins scrubbing again.)

SADIE: *(Sings)*
Hey there compass, bring me home…
Hey there compass, I'm all alone…
Once was lost…now I'm found…

(RO kicks the bag in boredom and sighs. SADIE scrubs some more, trying to ignore her.)

SADIE: *(Sings)*
Hey there compass, bring me home…
Hey there compass, I'm all alone—

(RO sighs louder kicking the bag around the room.)

SADIE: Must you do that?

RO: What?

SADIE: You know what?

RO: I'm not doing nothing—

SADIE: You know exactly what you're doing.

RO: Sorry.

(Silence)

SADIE: Thank you…

(SADIE attempts to scrub at the wall again. RO sighs louder this time.)

SADIE: LORD, HELP MY SOUL! Alright Alright I'll tell you…I'm searching for something.

(Pause)

RO: Searchin'? Searchin' for what?

SADIE: I don't rightly know…my life back—

(Pause)

RO: You're searchin' for your life back?

SADIE: Or something like that—

RO: Why?

SADIE: Cause I lost it.—

RO: Ma'am?

SADIE: Ummm…

RO: Why you dressed like that?

SADIE: Like what?

RO: Ain't you hot in your Sunday clothes like that?

SADIE: No child.

RO: Shit, I'm breakin' into a sweat just looking at you.

SADIE: Language!

RO: Hey, lady let me ask you something else?

SADIE: If I answer your question, will you shut up?

RO: Yeah sure, aight.

SADIE: Then what is it?

RO: I saw you take some medicine awhile ago…what are you some kinda pill poppin' freak or something?

Ro holds out the bottle of pills and shakes it.

SADIE: How'd you get that? Give me that back?

(SADIE snatches the pill away from RO.)

RO: Damn… Sorry, what are you taking these pills for anyway?

SADIE: Doctor says I got a weak heart, but I know the truth. Don't need no silly doctor tellin' me what's wrong. I got broken-heart disease. Doctor at this clinic gave me this lil' pill said it'll help ease my pain.

RO: What pain you got?

SADIE: Look around, child. Look around…this is my American dream. That's my pain…child.

RO: I don't get you lady… If it gives you so much pain, then what you doin' stay here for?

SADIE: Cause it's a part of me. It's etched deep in me. Every part of it… the good and the bad.

(Pause)

RO: If you say so…

(Pause)

This is a strange neighborhood though, I tell you that much. Seems like almost every house has been destroyed and deserted. Only people I've seen here is you and that smiling man, oh and the sky.

SADIE: What about the sky?

RO: It's a sky full of stars in the middle of day.

(Silence)

SADIE: You've noticed that, too?

RO: Don't see how anyone could miss it. Something about this place ain't quite right.

(Pause)

SADIE: It's nothing.

(Pause)

RO: Well, what about where all the people are at? All the houses look condemned or boarded up around here. And then there's that man?

SADIE: I don't know… Been here only a few days trying to piece this place back together when you came here. I'm curious you want to get into my business so much. Let's talk about you—

RO: What about me?

SADIE: What's your story, darling?

RO: I don't got no story.

SADIE: Everybody has a story, child.

RO: I'd rather not talk about it.

SADIE: Come on now, child. What did you say your name was? Age getting' to my memory… You said your name is Ro?

Ro fishes a cigarette and a lighter from her backpack.

RO: It's Roquisha LaBranch.

SADIE: Roquisha LaBranch.

RO: Yes

SADIE: LaBranch—

RO: Yeah. Roquisha LaBranch.

SADIE: Roquisha LaBranch?

RO: Would you stop repeating me?

(SADIE *walks over and takes the cigarette from* RO'*s hand.*)

RO: Hey, lady, what gives—

SADIE: We're going to stick with Ro, sweetheart. How old are you?

RO: Fifteen but I got an old soul.

SADIE: What you doing out here on your own any how?

RO: I'm…I can take care of myself.

SADIE: I can see that…especially since you got some strange man after you. Where's your people's at child?

RO: Look lady, I ain't no child—

SADIE: Sure fooled me—

RO: Yeah, whatever—

SADIE: I'm going to ask you again where's your family at?

RO: Gone.

SADIE: Now what do you mean gone?

RO: Gone…as in G-O-N… Gone.

SADIE: You know you not to young to get knocked out?
(*Pause*)
So you tellin' me, you don't have a home?

RO: Yeah, I got a home…I got a big home. Two stories,
with wood floors, and huge double doors, and lots of
windows to let in the sunlight.

SADIE: Then where your mother and father at?

RO: I got locked out the house is all.

SADIE: You got locked out your house? You can't call
nobody to let you back in?

RO: No ma'am.

SADIE: Where you're momma at?

RO: My mom, she's went to go march in a parade…
took the ferry to New Orleans on a first class ticket
gone for seven days…she'll be back for me. Listen,
lady…I'm fine. As soon as that man leaves. You won't
have to worry about me none.

SADIE: You let me worry about what I ought to worry
about.
What else you got in the bag?

RO: Damn you ask a lot of questions.

SADIE: I'm trying to help you.

RO: Why you care about me and my troubles anyway,
lady?

SADIE: What are your troubles?

RO: When did I say I had any?

SADIE: Baby girl, I think you just did… you just did…

RO: To hell with all this.

(She moves to the door to exit.)

SADIE: Watch your language, child.

(RO at the door when she sees the man still outside.)

(Pause)

RO: I'm calling it a night.

(Pause)

It's so cold in here. Where can I sleep?

SADIE: I made a bed from some old rags I found. I don't have a clue where you sleepin', child.

(She finds a way to get comfortable on the bed of rags and prepares to sleep.)

RO: Oh…aight. That's cool…I'll just make myself comfortable.

(RO curls herself into a ball and shifts restlessly in the corner of the room, trying to get comfortable. She fails. SADIE sighs in annoyance.)

SADIE: You can sleep here next to me if you'd like.

(Pause)

RO: Lady, I don't know you like that.

SADIE: I'm just making an offer.

(Pause… RO considers it.)

RO: You not going to try anything are you?

SADIE: You gonna make me change my mind in a minute. These floors here ain't exactly the most comfortable places to lie down. Broken glass, splinters all over… Lord know this not the ideal place to lie your head. Over here under these rags, they'll offer some comfort, but I ain't going to offer what you don't want.

RO: Alright then.

SADIE: Check the doors real fast see if that man still out there.

(RO *checks the doors and windows before lying down next to* SADIE.)

RO: He's out there.

SADIE: Well, I guess you can stay then.

RO: Thank you, lady.

(RO *and* SADIE *look at each other for a moment. Really look at each other. There is something familiar to them about each other.* RO *shakes out of it.*)

RO: What?

SADIE: God those eyes.

(*Pause*)

RO: You a real strange lady you know that?

(*Pause*)

(RO *goes back to sleep.* SADIE *quietly watches her.*)

SADIE: So you say...so you say...
(*She sings quietly to* RO.)
Hey there compass, bring me home...
Hey there compass, I'm all alone...
Once was lost...now I'm found...
Hey there compass, bring me home...
Hey there compass, I'm...

(SADIE *notices* RO's *asleep.*)

(*She observes her momentarily, then opens* RO's *backpack. She pulls out a teddy bear.*)

SADIE: I had a bear just like this when I was her age.

(SADIE *returns the small teddy bear to the bag and closes it before she moves towards the sleeping figure of* RO.)

(SADIE *sits on a pile of rags in the corner of the room.*)

SADIE: Who are you?

(She brushes the hair from her face.)

Why does it feel like I know you, child? Who you runnin' from? What you hidin', huh? I don't know why you here, but Baby you're not suppose to be here... Not here...

(She moves away from RO, *examining the walls that surround her.)*

What am I doing here, Lord? I don't know what I'm doing here.

*(*SADIE *hears the sound of a bell ringing out... Once... She stares outward as if trying to see outside.)*

SADIE: Who's there?

(The sound of a bell rings out again...once...twice...)

(Silence)

SADIE: Maybe it's just the night playin' with my mind.

*(*SADIE *moves to go to lie next to* RO *when she hears the bells again. Once...twice...three times.)*

SADIE: Who's there? I'm serious... Show your self now!

*(*CLARENCE *steps through the wall.)*

(He is dressed fashionably in a double breasted frock coat suit, with elephant bell trousers with seven inch cuffs and a half open shirt. Clearly he's wearing the finest of clothes from the 1970s... He's youthful and charming.)

SADIE: Is anybody there?

*(*CLARENCE *lights a cigar he's holding in his hands and approaches.)*

CLARENCE: Hey you.

SADIE: What do you want?

CLARENCE: Just you, Sadie Baby.

SADIE: How do you know my name? Who are you?

CLARENCE: You know who I am.

SADIE: No I don't.

CLARENCE: You don't know who I am? You don't recognize the man who use to kiss you on the forehead every night? You don't recognize the man who loved you and called you his wife?

SADIE: Clarence?!!

CLARENCE: It's been awhile since I heard my baby call out my name...say it again...

(SADIE *gasps for breath, she takes a pill. Waits...nothing happens...*)

SADIE: Clarence...Is that. Really. You?

CLARENCE: In the flesh, Sadie baby...well more or less... Go ahead and let me hear you say my name just once more...for good luck.

SADIE: I'm losing my mind...I'm seeing things...you're not real...you're not real—
(*She takes another pill.*)

CLARENCE: Sadie, it's me.

(*Pause*)

SADIE: This is not happening... This is not happening... this is not happening... You're just a figment of my imagination?

CLARENCE: Now, I've been called a lot of things by you, baby love, but that's a new one for the books.
(*Pause*)
Here, maybe this will help you.

(CLARENCE *holds out a tightly clenched fist and opens it slowly and* SADIE's *breathing calms, she takes a deep breath.*)

CLARENCE: Better?

(SADIE *jerks away in wonder.*)

SADIE: *(To herself)* Sadie May Jenkins, you listen to me… You're old, you're feeble, you're mind is slipping away in your final hours… This is not happening…

CLARENCE: Uh, baby, I don't know how to tell you this but…
It kinda is.

SADIE: Clarence, You're not real…

(CLARENCE pinches SADIE.)

SADIE: Ow, What did you do that for?

(SADIE smacks CLARENCE.)

CLARENCE: If I was a ghost could I do that?

SADIE: What you doing here? You got everybody thinking your dead, you know that?

CLARENCE: Good, just the way I like it.

(SADIE moves away from CLARENCE.)

SADIE: How can this be? I saw the house burn down…I saw the fire department pull you out of the rubble.

CLARENCE: I'm sorry, you had to see that.

SADIE: I identified you at the morgue. I saw you lying on that cold metal table only way I could tell it was you was cause of your wedding ring.

(CLARENCE raises his hand out and wiggles his finger showing the wedding ring.)

CLARENCE: This one?

SADIE: Sweet Jesus, How is this possible?

(SADIE notices CLARENCE's hands burnt and scarred.)

SADIE: Your hands?

CLARENCE: A reminder of where I've been.

SADIE: Does it hurt?

(CLARENCE shrugs.)

SADIE: So if you're alive… Where you been all this time?

CLARENCE: What's your definition of alive?

SADIE: Where you been, Clarence, Where. You. Been…?

(CLARENCE *takes a long look at* SADIE, *taking her in.*)

CLARENCE: I almost forgot how beautiful you are, when you're mad.
(He *suddenly notices the house.*)

SADIE: Don't change the subject. Where?

CLARENCE: Where's the closest place a man can get to heaven?

(Pause)

SADIE: Nawlins'?

CLARENCE: Nawlins', oh and it's beautiful over there. It's heaven, you should come see it.

SADIE: You're in Nawlin', then what you doing here?

CLARENCE: I came to see my Sadie Baby.

SADIE: What do you want?

CLARENCE: A brotha, can't come see the woman he loves?

SADIE: What you doing here?

CLARENCE: You just gonna make me come on out and say it then, huh?

SADIE: Well.

CLARENCE: Sadie, it hurt not seeing you deliver that eulogy at my funeral. Ain't nothin' hurt worse than seeing you do that.

SADIE: Good, cause it hurt watching our house burn down—

CLARENCE: Woman—

SADIE: Don't you woman me!

CLARENCE: You don't go say goodbye to your husband?

SADIE: Bye.

CLARENCE: Don't you turn around on me… Sadie, you could have at least come and said goodbye to me?

SADIE: Negro, you standing right there—

CLARENCE: Sadie, Sadie… Sadie, you know what I mean! See that's what's wrong with you women… they don't make sisters like they use to. A man is just that… Not perfect but a man…flawed, human and you women can't comprehend that.

Sadie waves her hand in disgust at Clarence.

CLARENCE: You can scoff if you want to—

SADIE: *(mocking Clarence)*

Well thank you for giving me permission…to scoff.

CLARENCE: You know… Use to be a time a woman would say here's a man…here's a good man, he might not be a great man, but I can help him get there.

(SADIE laughs.)

SADIE: Is that right?

CLARENCE: Yeah, that's right… Not now, expect a brother to be perfect or nothing at all…so when he falls on his ass, you don't let him pick himself up and try again.
Oh, no you'd rather banish that man into the darkness and never let him see the light.

SADIE: You set our house on fire, Clarence—

CLARENCE: Man messed up, you don't even give him a chance to repent. You got your mind made up and don't even half know what about, before you even hear where he at… Forgiveness is divine… Sadie, you Christian, you ought to know that.

SADIE: Clarence Elmore Jenkins, you going to make me throw something at you.

(Pause)

I can't do this…I ain't doing this with you now.

CLARENCE: Shit, why the hell not? I can't think of a better time than now.

SADIE: Watch your language.

(CLARENCE waves his hands in disgust mocking SADIE's previous gesture.)

(CLARENCE notices the sleeping figure of RO.)

CLARENCE: Question? Who she?

SADIE: Will you keep it down, she's sleeping.

CLARENCE: Who's the girl?

SADIE: Shhh—

CLARENCE: Woman, I know you didn't just shhh, me…

(Pause)

What she doing here?

SADIE: It's not your concern.

CLARENCE: Hell yes, its' my concern.

Clarence steps back, trying to make sense of things.

CLARENCE: *(Mutters to himself)* Now that just doesn't make any sense—

SADIE: What doesn't make sense?

CLARENCE: What? Oh nothing.

SADIE: You just said…

CLARENCE: No. I. No…It nothing… Never you mind.

(Pause)

So…

SADIE: So?

CLARENCE: Just out of curiosity? Don't you have enough children, huh? Three sons, five grandbabies with another on the way… You're going to end up like that story about the old woman that lived in the shoe. You know the one don't ya?

SADIE: Stop.

CLARENCE: What… What?

SADIE: It don't concern you none.

CLARENCE: It concerns me that you got some strange lil' be-be kid sleepin' in my house… Who is she?
(Silence)
Answer me!

SADIE: Oh no, you not comin' into my house askin' questions!

CLARENCE: It's my house, too.

SADIE: Negro, I don't have to explain nothing to you, in sickness and health, till death do us part…if my memory ain't mistaken, you dead.

CLARENCE: You're still wearing my ring aren't you? Then guess what? We're still married.

SADIE: I can take off the ring anytime.

CLARENCE: Then take it off.

SADIE: What?

CLARENCE: You heard me.

(Pause)

SADIE: Maybe I will.

CLARENCE: Go on then…take it off.

(SADIE begins to take the ring off her finger and then stops.)

SADIE: I don't want to.

CLARENCE: That's what I thought.
(To the sleeping RO.*)*
Psst...psst... Hey you... Lil' girl... Hey lil' girl...wake up...what the hell you doing in my house?

*(*SADIE *tries to wave* CLARENCE *to the door.)*

SADIE: She's sleeping... Can you just respect that? For once in your life can you respect something?

CLARENCE: Oh, don't be like that—

SADIE: Like what?

CLARENCE: Like this...
(Pause)
Why you being stubborn, woman?

SADIE: I have to do this for me.

CLARENCE: How's playin' momma going to help you?
(Pause)
Well?

(Silence)

SADIE: That girl came into my life for a reason. She needs me.

CLARENCE: Hell, I need you woman. Look at her, she's a lil' hood rat, I bet she comes into a lot of peoples lives. Then I bet she kills them while they sleepin'.

SADIE: Now that's just being ridiculous.

CLARENCE: Am I? Am I really? Think about it, what do you really know about this girl?
(Pause)

SADIE: All that matters is she's in need... Now, are you done?

*(*CLARENCE *sighs. They both look at* RO *sleeping. They share a moment of silence. He finally shakes his head in disapproval.)*

CLARENCE: No, I'm not done—

SADIE: Lord have mercy.

(Pause)

CLARENCE: Look around you, what business you got taking in street rats?

SADIE: She has a name. So I thank you very much if you would use it instead of calling her a bunch of names, and it's Ro La Branch.

(There is a moment of silence, before CLARENCE *laughs.)*

SADIE: What's so funny?

(Pause)

CLARENCE: Her name is LaBranch?

SADIE: Yes.

(Pause)

CLARENCE: LaBranch… Like the street?

(Pause)

SADIE: Yes.

(Pause)

CLARENCE: Like the street you grew up on?

SADIE: Yes Clarence…yes.

*(*CLARENCE *laughs.)*

CLARENCE: Woman, that ain't her name, she's playing you for a sucker.

(Silence)

SADIE: Bye Clarence.

(Pause)

CLARENCE: God, look at this place. Come here let me hold you. I haven't felt your arms around me in what seems like an eternity…

(SADIE *doesn't move.*)

CLARENCE: I missed you, Sadie, come here and hold me again, hold me tight, that's all I want.

SADIE: Is that all you want?

CLARENCE: After forty three years of marriage, you know I can't live without that touch of yours.

(*Pause*)

SADIE: Forty four.

CLARENCE: What?

SADIE: Clarence, I've been married to you for forty four years.

(*Pause*)

CLARENCE: Forty three…forty four…you know what I mean, that's not the point.

SADIE: The point is, when you say that's all you want, We both know, you want more than what you say.

CLARENCE: Just give me a hug, Sadie Baby…

(SADIE *gives in.* CLARENCE *and* SADIE *embrace.*)

(CLARENCE *holds on longer than* SADIE *wants. She slips away.*)

CLARENCE: There now, was that so much to ask for?

(SADIE *notices* CLARENCE's *chest is burnt and scarred.*)

(*She touches it…*)

SADIE: Your chest.

CLARENCE: The stories these marks could tell. Listen Sadie, I'm startin' up a new life in Nawlins'… A good life.
I want you to join me. I got you a ticket so you can take the ferry over; it's only good for one. First Class.

(CLARENCE *takes out a ticket and places it in* SADIE's *hand.*)

SADIE: Clarence.

CLARENCE: You should see the place. It's a classy joint, baby, real classy…just simple people live there, good people.

You'd like it there, everything you thought mattered, don't… It's how you live your life that matters…that's it. Christian, Arabs, Jews…everyone, everything… Hell, even white people up over there getting a chance to make themselves a good life. Each and everyone accepted. Puts a whole new spin on Affirmative Action, baby.

SADIE: Sounds, nice.

CLARENCE: It is baby. Oh, and guess what?!! I got a job.

SADIE: You haven't worked a single day since you retired from construction work.

CLARENCE: Yeah, but I'm working now, Sadie…I'm the Book.

SADIE: You got a job as a book-keeper? You're horrible with numbers.

CLARENCE: But I'm great with names though…you're looking at the one and only Book.

SADIE: Book, How you going to be a book?

CLARENCE: The mayor said he had a job for me… Told me he was impressed. Said not many would do what I did nowadays. Can you believe I impressed The Mayor? I'm his new *Book of Life* he signed me up the day my sun had set…

SADIE: Clarence.

(Silence)

CLARENCE: The point is, come back with me, Sadie, just tell me what I got to do to get you to come back with me. We got the chance to start over.

(Pause)

*(*SADIE *doesn't answer.)*

CLARENCE: So, if that girl wasn't here would you come with me?

SADIE: Why? Do you plan to give me a home again, Clarence?

CLARENCE: If that's what I got to do then that's what I'll do. In the mean time, be careful around here until I get back, something not quite right around here.
(He exits, vanishes through the wall he entered through.)

*(*RO *stirs and awakens.)*

RO: Hey lady?

SADIE: Yes, angel? What do you want, darling?

RO: It sounded like there was a man in here. Were you just talking to someone?

*(*SADIE's *hand still clutches the ticket.)*

SADIE: Darling, not a soul here but me.

(She stands alone. She lets the ticket fall to the floor.)

(End scene)

Scene 3:
The Neighborhood Watch

(The next day. Morning. RO *sleeps;* SADIE *is gone… A man [*SMILES*] pushing aside some of the rubble waits for her.)*

(He sits there quietly for a moment, then clears his throat.)

(Ro wakes up, turns and sees the strange man smiling at her.)

(His name fits him.)

SMILES: Roses or lilacs?

Ro: What? How'd you get in here?

Smiles: I'm trying to figure out what it is that you smell like. It's a sweet smell. I like it…

Ro: Who the hell are you?

Smiles: Oh you know who I am? Don't you?

Ro: You're him.

Smiles: Mmm hmm…

Ro: You're the man that was following me?

Smiles: You have something I want… Give it to me?

Ro: What are you talkin' about? No I don't.

Smiles: Maybe I should rephrase that statement. You don't exactly how should I put it…belong here…and I want to know…
Who are you? What are you doing here? And most importantly how'd you get here?

Ro: I…umm, look, I'm sorry I can't help you…

(Ro *moves to leave,* Smiles *stops her.*)

Smiles: Tell me and I'll go back on my way.

Ro: I don't know what you're talkin' about.

Smiles: Well, maybe I was mistaken…

Ro: Yeah, well maybe you were… Why were you following me?

Smiles: I hope I didn't scare you. I'm the neighborhood watch. I saw you from across the street.
I could smell you from blocks away…I figured I should come see what was going on over here.

Ro: Who are you?

Smiles: Where are my manners? They call me Smiles.

Ro: Just Smiles?

Smiles: Just Smiles…And you what's your name?

RO: Ro…

SMILES: It's just Ro?

RO: Just Ro.

SMILES: You're very pretty, you know that?

RO: What you want?

SMILES: Now, you don't gotta be like that, I'm just trying to pay you a lil' compliment. You the only one here, girl?

SADIE: No, she's not, what do you want?

(The sound of the back door barricade being pushed aside: SADIE enters from the back of the house. She carries a basket of rotten fruit.)

(She looks first at SMILES and then at RO, before finally turning her attention back towards the smiling intruder.)

RO: I swear I didn't let this man in here.

SADIE: Everything is going to be alright…I'm here now.

SMILES: I know you… Ain't you the old woman who use to live here?

SADIE: I'm the old woman who does live here.

SMILES: Yeah, I remember you. You're Mrs Jenkins… I know you. You're husband lost his mind and set the house on fire, charbroiled himself while doing it, right? Yeah I remember all about that… What an unfortunate tragedy. My heart wept for you when I heard that.

SADIE: Thank you, what can I do for you?

SMILES: Straight to the point…I like that, got to respect that. Definitely got to respect that…I don't mean to take time out you, ladies, busy schedule, see I'm part of the neighborhood watch committee. I was hoping that I might get the chance to speak with you in private.

SADIE: We don't have nothing to give. I'm sorry.

Wish I could help you.

SMILES: No…no…no…not askin' for any support of the financial kind whatsoever. See we need your help Mrs Jenkins.

Help us continue our work of protecting the neighborhood from…unwanted elements.

SADIE: I'm listenin', start talkin'.

(SMILES *pulls out a cigarette.*)

SMILES: You want your streets safe right?

SADIE: Right.

SMILES: Everybody needs that peace of mind. I'd hate for another tragedy to come your direction because you didn't do your part. These old houses, they've been known to catch fire unexpectedly. You don't mind if I smoke do you?

SADIE: Actually, I'd like it if you'd put that out…

(*Pause*)

SMILES: Oh sorry, now where are my manners?
(*He puts out the cigarette.*)

SADIE: Thank you.

SMILES: Mind if I ask you Mrs. Jenkins, who's the little girl to you?

(*Pause*)

SADIE: She's… She's my daughter. Isn't that right, Ro?

RO: What?

SADIE: Your my daughter aren't you, Ro?

RO: Ummm…damn straight…I mean, yes, Mama Jenkins.

SMILES: Of course…I did not know you had a daughter. I see it now; she has your eyes. Again Mrs. Jenkins, I hope you don't mind me asking but may I speak to you in private.

RO: Anything, you got to say to her, might as well come right on out and say it now... Cause me and her, we're like this...

SADIE: Ro...go on outside.

RO: But...

SADIE: Ro

RO: But that's the man that's been following me.

SADIE: Outside...

RO: But that's him...

SADIE: Silence, child! Let me talk to the nice man.

RO: But he's...

SADIE: Don't make me repeat myself. I need to talk to the Neighborhood Watch. It's important. Isn't it, Mister?...

SMILES: Smiles.
(Pause)
Just Smiles.

(RO exits warily.)

SADIE: State your business.

SMILES: Might want to keep an eye on your daughter, Mrs Jenkins.

SADIE: And why's that?

SMILES: There's been things turning up missing in the neighborhood lately. Lost...stolen perhaps.

SADIE: I got no reason to steal.

SMILES: Of course not you, you're a respected member of this community... But it wasn't you I was referring to...

SADIE: Then what you getting at?

SMILES: Your ummm…your daughter, do you know where she was yesterday morning?

(Pause)

SADIE: She was with me…

SMILES: I wonder about that…the store cross the way says a girl came in and stole food. Said they'd seen her run this way.

SADIE: That's funny, been a long time since I've seen a soul in this neighborhood.

SMILES: Oh they're around.

SADIE: What does Ro have to steal for?

SMILES: I don't know…she's your daughter?

SADIE: You suppose to be the policeman around here?

SMILES: Just a concern citizen. I'd hate to bring the police into this though…what would happen if I pointed them in the direction of this house? What would they think if they found out a sweet old lady like you was living alone in a place like this? They'd put you away somewhere. Imagine what type of hell you could be living in.

SADIE: You wouldn't do that…would you?

SMILES: I'd never do something like that. After all, we have to look out for each other in this neighborhood. Think things over. I'll be around let me know if you have anything for me. Can't let the unwanted elements just run the streets. We all want to feel safe don't we?

SADIE: That's what we have the neighborhood watch for isn't it? Help, make sure that we can all feel… safe.

SMILES: Of course. You have a lovely afternoon. Oh, Mrs. Jenkins, you should try smiling sometime it's good for your soul.

(He leaves.)

(End scene)

Scene 4:
Strange Dreams

(It's afternoon. RO enters carrying a small bowl of beans and rice. She sees SADIE, who sits staring into the darkness, murmuring to herself over and over again:)

SADIE: Don't leave me. Don't leave me.

RO: Hey lady? Hey lady, you alright?

(No response.)

RO: Is everything okay? Can you hear me?

(No response)

RO: Hey, Lady, wake up…you're freakin' me out here.

(No response)

(RO approaches SADIE, nudges her.)

RO: Hey, you alright?

(SADIE looks up at RO startled and cringes as RO stands over her.)

SADIE: Lord, have mercy. You gave me a fright.

RO: Gave you a fright? Shit you freaked me out!

SADIE: Ro, child you and that language of yours. I swear…

RO: What just happened?

SADIE: I don't know… Went off somewhere didn't I?

RO: Yeah you did, then you woke up and…

(Pause)

SADIE: And?

RO: Dang, lady, you look like I was about kill you or something. You was like that when I woke up, figured you was praying or something... Did you sleep at all?

SADIE: I don't.

RO: Oh, well... Morning anyway...I almost never seem to be able to sleep. But I slept on those rags you got piled up... Surprised me, slept like I was lying on clouds or something. I forget the saying. Hey, you hungry? This place is off the chain. I was standing here by the front door pacing, looking out the window, trying to see if I would see the strange man...and I was thinking to myself...

"Ro, I'm hungry". I kept looking out the window and as I kept pacing I heard this little voice saying "I'm hungry.", and I realized that the voice was me, saying, "I'm hungry".

I'm saying that over and over. Talking to myself like those old people often do... Not like you old but like old-old.

SADIE: You bothering me to tell me you were hungry?

RO: Anyway, so as this thought was going through my head, I hear something tell me go to the back door...I go to it. I open the door and there is no one there except a picnic basket. I open it, not sure what to expect...and get this...there is a bowl of rice and beans just sitting there... Can you believe that rice and beans? You want some?

SADIE: You opened the door?!!

RO: Somebody was knockin'.

SADIE: Girl, you must be part stupid? Don't open that door for nobody.

RO: But someone was there. Sorry won't do it again... just figured I should offer. You okay, you don't look so good?

SADIE: Just had a strange dream, or at least it felt like one...you were in it, angel. Dreamed we were surrounded by darkness and you and me stood alone on a platform high above a lake of fire. Then slowly the platform spiraled its way downward toward this... This place with nothing but pain and misery... And we're spiraling downwards and I see a light through the darkness and a hand reaches down and offers itself to us.

But it can only take one of us; the other must live in this lake of fire forever.

RO: Then what happened, who was pulled up?

SADIE: I don't know.

RO: Are you sure you don't want to share this?

SADIE: No, darling you go on ahead and eat.

RO: You, alright?

SADIE: Dream just troubled me a bit.

RO: You should eat at least some of this.
(She sits down and takes a bite from the bowl of food. She savors the taste.)
It's good... It's soul food. It's good for the soul...

SADIE: I ain't hungry.

(Silence)

RO: Hey ummm... What did you and that smiling man talk about?

(Pause)

(SADIE begins gasping for breath again.)

SADIE: Concern yourself with what you need to concern yourself with.

RO: Are you alright?

SADIE: I'm fine…just need to take my medication that's all.

(She reaches into her purse and pulls out her pills and takes one. Her breathing calms. She rocks back and forth.)

RO: Alright, if you say so… Hey, thank you for lettin' me stay here… not many people would let a stranger stay with them.

SADIE: Well, we all come into each others lives for a reason.

RO: I guess.

(Pause)

Say lady, why you let me stay here? You hardly know me.

(Pause)

SADIE: I don't know.

(Pause)

(SADIE continues to rock back and forth. As she does the graffittied writing that has been revealed on the wall start to glow. She notices but says nothing.)

SADIE: I honestly don't rightly know.

RO: You know lady, for someone as old as you are there seems to be a lot you don't know.

Child, the older you get the more you realize that fact is true.

RO: I guess…

(Pause)

Oh hey, you plannin' on going somewhere?

SADIE: No why?

RO: Well, then what's Charon Ferry Service? You got a first class ticket. I found this on the floor when I woke up.

(She reaches into her back pocket and pulls out the ticket that CLARENCE *handed* SADIE *earlier.)*

SADIE: Give that here.

*(*SADIE *takes it out of* RO's *hand and the writing fades. She places the ticket into her pocket.)*

(Silence)

RO: Well, hey ummm…I looked outside today and didn't see that man out there…

SADIE: You plannin' on leavin'?

RO: Well, yeah.

SADIE: Where would you go?

RO: The opposite of here would be…oh yeah, out there.

SADIE: There's nothing out there…

RO: Yeah, well I think I'll take my chances.

SADIE: Wait up, lil' girl.

RO: I ain't no little girl.

*(*SADIE *laughs…)*

SADIE: Sure fooled me… Ain't you a little old for teddy bears?

*(*RO *steps back. Her face drops.)*

RO: How you know…?

(Pause)

SADIE: Why you out on these streets like this?

RO: You don't know me.

SADIE: I know you're lost…

RO: What you know? Huh? What do ya know? Look lady, I ain't lost. I know exactly where I am.

SADIE: Do you really? Where's your family, girl?

RO: I told you…

SADIE: Where your family, child?

RO: What does it matter? Where's yours?

SADIE: Burned away.

RO: That why you look so pitiful?

SADIE: What you talkin' about?

RO: You look pitiful.

SADIE: Pitiful… Who pitiful? I'm not pitiful.

RO: You look just plain old pitiful and lonely to me… I ain't seen you smile since I've been here. What you livin' in this place for?

(Silence)

(SADIE and RO turn their back on each other. They sigh and fold their arms in unison.)

RO: *(Mutters to herself)* Pitiful if you ask me… You're nothing but a pitiful old woman living in a pitiful old burnt down house…and you got the nerve to judge me. Please.

(Pause)

SADIE: What you say?

RO: Nothing.

SADIE: No…no…no…what did you say to me?

RO: I wasn't talking to you.

SADIE: But you were talkin' about me. You want to say something, then say something. We're all grown here aren't we?!!

RO: I said you're nothing but a pitiful old lonely crazy woman!!! And I pray to God, I don't end nothing like you.

(SADIE raises her hand to slap RO. But stops herself. They both recoil. They look at each other.)

(Silence)

(RO *realizes the mistake she's made and tries to apologize.*)

RO: I'm sorry.

SADIE: I don't need no child judging me.

RO: Hey look I'm...I'm sorry, alright. I'm just sayin'.

SADIE: I think you've said enough. I don't need nobody pryin' into my business. Come to think of it you're right.
(She moves to the door.)

RO: Wait, where you going?

SADIE: I'm not going anywhere, maybe you right... maybe I don't know you. Maybe I don't need to know you...
(She takes RO's backpack.)

RO: Hey lady, put down my bag?

SADIE: Shame really, cause I wanted to help you, but maybe you right. I got my burdens I don't need yours as well.

RO: Put down my bag...

SADIE: So here's what we're going to do? I'm going to go my way...you go on and go yours...
(She drops RO's bag by the door.)
(Pause)
I ain't got no business trying to protect no child.

RO: So what am I suppose to do?

SADIE: Whatever you want child, don't concern me...I did my part.

RO: Aight that's my cue to leave. Fine...nice meeting you. Not.

(SADIE *reconsiders things, as* RO *moves to exit.*)

SADIE: I just hope that man don't come back. You and him by yourselves. That could be a horrible shame…to think about what could happen to you.

RO: What do you mean?

SADIE: He could kill you…you could die…

RO: I could die?

SADIE: Or worse.

(Pause)

RO: Worse?

SADIE: Oh yeah angel, there are worse fates than death.

RO: Worse than death?

SADIE: Far worse. But if you want to go out there far be it from me to stop you…you grown. Take care of yourself now?

RO: So if I stay here what would we do?

(End scene)

Scene 5:
Searching for that Smile

(The same day. Early afternoon)

(SADIE scrubs at the wall fiercely revealing more words, as RO sorts through the box.)

SADIE: All this damn writing on the wall, why would anybody do this?

RO: Language…

SADIE: What? Uh, oh child…you got me.

RO: So all this wasn't on the wall before the fire?

SADIE: Why would I do this to my own home, child?

RO: I don't know… Feng shui the joint, give it a little flava maybe.

(Pause)

SADIE: You think you're funny?

RO: No ma'am…
(She sorts items into boxes. She pulls out one item followed by another then another.)

RO: Hey lady, is this what you're looking for?

SADIE: No…

RO: This it?

SADIE: No…

RO: This it?

SADIE: Ummm…wait… It could be? Is it?
(Pause)
No.

RO: What exactly is it we're looking for?

SADIE: I'll know it when I see it…

RO: So you don't even know what it looks like?

SADIE: You'll know it when I know it…

(RO pulls out a photograph charred around the edges. SADIE stops as she sees RO holding it in her hand.)

RO: What's wrong?

SADIE: Memories just stirrin' up?

RO: Let me see… He's handsome. Who's that?

SADIE: Some things you just can't shake loose.
(She takes the photograph.)

RO: What you mean?

SADIE: Love has healing power, but it can be a deadly poison too.

RO: He the reason you're so sad?

SADIE: He's no one…

RO: Why would you say that?

SADIE: Cause there's nothing to say about him, child.

(RO *stares at* SADIE.)

RO: Please?

SADIE: You see this picture right here?

RO: Yes, ma'am…

SADIE: That's all I got to remind me I had a past once. Clarence, my husband took that picture in Nawlins'. Told me if Heaven was on earth and man could just walk into it, it would be Nawlin'. You know something dear. I use to walk these streets just like you. Mad at everybody and everything I saw until I met him. I was maybe about your age, maybe a little older. Clarence was well… He was no saint, but he was an angel of a man… He was something to see, smooth brown skin, tall and when he walked into a room, child, you knew you were looking at a man. Ah, and his smile, that man's smile could swallow you whole. He walked up to me, I remember it clearly, He stood looking at me, said he would do anything to make me smile and I believed him. I opened my heart to him. Gave him everything he ever wanted. Gave him three boys, and you know how he proved his love to me? Forty four years later, the man loved me so much he set our house on fire with him inside. Does that sound like the thing a man would do that loves you?

RO: No. No it don't.

Clarence appears, his hat in hand. Only Sadie sees him.

SADIE: That's what I said as well. So when I stood to eulogize him before we placed him in the ground, I found that I couldn't speak. Every wonderful moment

we shared was burned up. The birth of our three
children. Our marriage. The life we shared. All up
in flames like it didn't matter anymore. The nights
he held me tight and he whispered that everything
would be alright. Burned away. His gentle kiss on the
forehead soothing the pain I felt from long days.
Burned away. Him singing me to sleep. Burned away.
I stood there at that funeral, with all those people
waiting for me to tell that man goodbye and say why I
was going to miss him, and I couldn't. All I could see
was this house burning away my love.

RO: Is that why you live here? Like this?

(CLARENCE *fades away.*)

SADIE: I told you more than you need to know.

(SADIE *continues to scrub at the walls occasionally stopping
to stare out a shattered window or out the door checking to
see if she spots Smiles. She sings to herself.*)

(*As she does the walls once again begins to glow.*)

SADIE: (*Sings*)
Hey there compass, bring me home…
Hey there compass, I'm all alone…
Hey there compass, bring me home…
Hey there compass, I'm all alone…

RO: What are you singing?

SADIE: A song.

RO: Why you sing that song?

SADIE: Every song got a memory…I sing this one cause
I can't find myself any kind of peace…I just keep
hoping that, maybe I'll find it in that song.

RO: What you mean? How do you know when you
finally find that?

(SADIE*'s eyes turn vacant, her mind on something unseen.
She begins to whisper the words:*)

SADIE: Don't leave me. *(Over and over)*

(Silence)

RO: Mama Jenkins? Mama Jenkins?

SADIE: Yes, Ro?

(Pause)

I faded off again didn't I?

RO: Where do you go to when you do that?

(Pause)

SADIE: Sometimes I'm dreaming...I don't know where I am. I'm laying in a white room somewhere, and my boys sitting around me, tears in their eyes. Then as fast as it comes, I'm back here.

(The illuminated writing starts to fade out again.)

(Silence)

SADIE: I don't understand you, child, why don't you go to that big two stories home of yours, with the family that loves and cares for you... Why don't you go back to that?

RO: Home? Go back to that home! What home, lady? That don't exist for me...

SADIE: But you said...

RO: That ain't never existed for me! That's why I can't go back to that... Shit! That's just a dream...

SADIE: Thought you said...

RO: I know what I said. I ain't got no family! I ain't got shit!

SADIE: You lied to me.

RO: Well, now you know. There are you happy?

SADIE: What else you lie about? Where you get the food earlier?

RO: Mind your own business, you old witch.

SADIE: What you say to me? You forget this is my place, child.

Watch what you say to me or I'll snatch you up so quick, your soul won't be able to figure out which way is heaven and hell. You hear me?

RO: No, you heard me…I call you an old…

(SADIE *slap* RO, RO's *shocked.*)

(*Silence*)

RO: I'm gone.

(*Pause*)

SADIE: Ro wait.

(*Pause*)

Don't you dare. Child…Ro…where are you going? Don't you leave this house… You walk out that door don't think of coming back…come back…

(RO *exits.*)

SADIE: Ro! Ro come back here!

She'll come back… She'll be back… Please come back…
(*She sits there in silence.*)

END OF ACT ONE

ACT TWO
Saint Sadie May Jenkins

Scene 1:
Waiting Room

(Late at night)

*(*SADIE *paces the room.)*

(Once…twice…three times the bell rings.)

SADIE: Oh, Lord my soul… not now.

*(*CLARENCE *enters dancing, dressed in flashy colorful three-piece suit carrying an equally colorful Mardi Gras umbrella. A New Orleans style jazz band plays in the background.)*

CLARENCE: *(Singing)*
Oh when the saints… Go marchin' in…
Oh when the saints go marchin' in…
Oh how I want to be in that number.
When them saints go marchin' in…

*(*CLARENCE *dances around a little bit more before he notices* SADIE.)*

CLARENCE: Hey Sadie baby!!! You miss me?!!

SADIE: What you doing here, Clarence?

CLARENCE: I came to see my Sadie Baby. You're missing out on one heck of a party up there, you know that? You'd love it.

SADIE: I'm not going nowhere, Clarence.

CLARENCE: *(Sighs)* I wish I had torn this damn house down… Torn this place down till there was nothing left for you to crawl into and trap yourself inside of, like this.

SADIE: I'm not in the mood.

CLARENCE: What's a matter lose your Lost Girl?

SADIE: Stop gloating it doesn't become you. She'll be back.

CLARENCE: Maybe she won't.

SADIE: Don't even know why I'm talkin' to you.

CLARENCE: Sadie sit down, you look like a nervous wreck.

SADIE: Why hasn't she came back yet? She's been gone for hours.

CLARENCE: I don't know why you feel drawn to this girl.

SADIE: You wouldn't understand Clarence.

CLARENCE: Try me.

SADIE: She…
(Pause)
She ain't got no family.

CLARENCE: You're concerned with matters that ain't important

SADIE: Ain't important?

CLARENCE: You heard me.

SADIE: And you're the judge of what is important?

CLARENCE: I don't judge. That's not in my job description…I'm just sayin'…you need to figure out what's important to you and that girl ain't on that list.

SADIE: What are you saying?

CLARENCE: I'm saying me or Little Orphan Annie.

SADIE: It all makes sense to me now.

CLARENCE: About damn time.

SADIE: My Clarence wouldn't say something like that. I don't know what standing before me now. You're not my Clarence?

CLARENCE: Sadie…

SADIE: I can see it, I can see it, I can see it clear as day. You're a demon.

CLARENCE: I'm a demon now?

SADIE: Demon…

CLARENCE: Do I have any horns on my head? See a tail wagging behind me? See cloven hoofed feet, a pitchfork and flames burstin' from my ass. No… Then I'm no demon. I'm not a nightmare…I'm not a devil… I'm Clarence. The same man you married.

SADIE: In order for me to go to Nawlin, that means you want me to die.

CLARENCE: I never said die.

SADIE: Come go to Nawlin' with me…of course, I should have seen it.

CLARENCE: I want what's best for you.

SADIE: Best for me?

CLARENCE: Best for us.

SADIE: You're a devil…an angel of death, come to take me to hell.

CLARENCE: Now you done lost your damn mind.

SADIE: Have I really?

CLARENCE: Sadie, you don't get it! Why do you think no one walks these streets? Why do you think the sky is full of stars during broad daylight? This place may not be hell, but it's one stop away. Let me help you... Let me save you... Let me finish tearing this place down. Let me help you before it's too late. Listen to me love, things are happening, things beyond my control. And if you stay here any longer you're going to be stuck in the middle of something horrible.

SADIE: Oh, no... Clarence, or whoever you are...you not welcomed in my house. Here you left this.

(SADIE *pulls out the ticket and holds it out to* CLARENCE.)

CLARENCE: Come on don't do this...

SADIE: No.

CLARENCE: Sadie...

SADIE: I don't want nothing to do with you. You're the farthest to the thing that I want.

CLARENCE: You called me here.

SADIE: Well, I dialed the wrong number.

CLARENCE: Sadie, come back to Nawlins' with me. You're wanted there... you're needed there. Baby, I even did what you wanted me to do.

SADIE: I didn't tell you to do nothing.

Clarence takes off a gold necklace around his neck, which holds a golden key. He offers it to Sadie.

CLARENCE: In Nawlin' there are many mansions and you should see ours. You should see it, baby, oh, it's gorgeous. Just the way you always wanted it. This is my best work yet. Every inch of it built with love. Two stories big, Beautiful wood floors made from cypress trees, big French doors, plenty of windows to let the sun in and a nice cover patio with a swing to sit on... it's just like how you always wanted it, baby.

SADIE: Clarence.

CLARENCE: It's beautiful, but it's empty… It just needs you with me.

(CLARENCE *places the key into* SADIE's *hands. Closes her fingers over the key)*

CLARENCE: Come home with me, Sadie Baby, come see our new home.
(Silence)
What's here? Ruins? What kind of life is that for you? What's here for you, woman, answer me that?

SADIE: Everything you destroyed with gasoline and a match is here. Everything, Clarence… Everything… That's what's here.
And I'm going to find it once again in this house.
Cause you burned us away.

CLARENCE: Listen to what you're saying?

SADIE: I'm saying, I have to figure out what's left of me…
(Pause)
I have to find my smile.

CLARENCE: What does that even mean? Through helping some lost girl.

SADIE: I can see her for who she is…I got the eyes to see her.

CLARENCE: See her like you see me? Shit, I ain't looked this good since Nixon.

SADIE: That's not nice, Clarence.

CLARENCE: I'm trying to help you…

SADIE: How is forcing me out of my home, my house, the only thing I have left on this earth helping me?

CLARENCE: I'm not forcing you to do anything.

SADIE: Sounds like it to me…

CLARENCE: I'm trying to do what's best for you.

SADIE: You're trying to tear down this house...you're trying to tear down this house... When it's still stands... Scarred, ravaged, pillaged, and picked apart it still stands and I won't let you.

CLARENCE: Think about this, Sadie, think about this.

SADIE: Did you for one damn second think when you set our house on fire with you in it?

(CLARENCE *turns to leave. He stops.*)

CLARENCE: I'm not willing to let you go. I love you, Sadie. Our kind of love only comes once in a lifetime. You know it and I know it. Look at this as a second chance for us to start a new life together. A better life together.

SADIE: A better life together? Really is that what we'll find?

CLARENCE: Don't our love mean anything, baby?

SADIE: I love you Clarence...I always will love you... Even when I wanted to hate you, I couldn't put out this fire I got inside. I loved you with so much of me, I burned away till I became someone I don't recognize no more...I have to live in it. Not you...

CLARENCE: Sadie please.

SADIE: You just don't get it do you?

CLARENCE: I just want you Sadie... The woman I love... That's all I want. Come home with me.

SADIE: Take you're ticket and your key back, the woman I am now, is not getting on no ferry ride to Nawlins', not with you.

(SADIE *places the ticket and the key back into* CLARENCE's *hands.*)

(RO *enters with teddy bear clutched tightly in her arms.*)

RO: Hey Mama Jenkins?! You here?!!

(CLARENCE *drops the ticket and disappears.*)

RO: Hey Mama Jenkins.

SADIE: You came back?

(*Pause*)

RO: Ummm… Who were you talking to?

SADIE: Nobody…

RO: Are you alright?

SADIE: I'm fine…
(*She drops to her knees, she struggles to breathe. She struggles to find her pills.*)

RO: No your not…here let me help you.

SADIE: I thought I saw my Clarence.

RO: That's not possible. He's gone.

SADIE: I know but I saw him.

RO: Look lady, I know you probably require some kinda shrink, but I ain't the one that can help with that.
(*Pause*)
Listen, the dead don't come back. Plain and simple. Say it with me.

SADIE/RO: The dead don't come back…

RO: Right, no such thing as ghosts…
You're just tired that's all it is.

(RO *finds* SADIE *her pills and hands one to her.*)

You should get some sleep.

SADIE: I don't sleep Ro…I'm glad you came back though.

RO: Me too.

(*Pause*)

SADIE: What made you come back?

(Pause)

RO: I missed you.

SADIE: That man was out there wasn't he?

RO: That too.

SADIE: Thought so.

RO: Something not right with this place. Seemed like I walked for hours and every block I turned on lead me right back to here. Look, Mama Jenkins…I just want to apologize…

SADIE: Oh you do?

RO: Yeah.

SADIE: I'm listening.

RO: You've been really kind to me to let me stay here and I'm sorry I called you…

SADIE: An old crazy pitiful witch?

(Pause)

RO: I called you a witch?

SADIE: Yeah you did.

RO: Yeah then I apologize for that too…and I was wondering if…

SADIE: Yes, Ro?

RO: I got to do a lot of thinkin' wandering these streets. And I realized I don't know as much as I thought I did. Will you teach me… Tell me the things you wish someone had told you when you were young.

(SADIE laughs and shakes her head. She rises to her feet. Turns to walk away)

SADIE: Oh child, child, child…

RO: No serious, tell me… Please.

SADIE: Come here. Sit by me.

(RO *sits down beside* SADIE.)

SADIE: What brought this along?

RO: I don't know… Just a need… just a want to know.

(SADIE *closes her eyes and takes a deep breathe. She looks* RO *in the eyes. As she speaks one by one the words written upon the wall begin to illuminate, to fill the room with light and color.*)

SADIE: I wish someone had told me when I was young…I would have told her… Don't be afraid to struggle. I would tell her to trust herself…to love as much as you can…

I would have said to save pennies, and avoid credit cards and men with great smiles cause they're the devil…I would have told her to get out and see the world, and don't be trapped in this ghetto, that not every man that smiles at you loves you, and the ones that do love you, you should hold to them even if they fail you sometimes cause love is scarce.

I would say that she really is as great and beautiful as she thinks she is. That when someone knocks her down, stand back up, I would tell her…I would tell her that nothing in this world is worth losing your soul over and above all else that life is weaker than death, and death is far weaker than love.

(*The graffiti writing once again fade away.*)

(*And* RO *and* SADIE *find themselves once again in the shadowy darkness of the burnt out shotgun house.*)

SADIE: I want you to tell me something, Ro. I want you to be honest.

RO: Alright.

SADIE: Did you steal that food?

(*Pause*)

RO: I found it by the door steps I swear it.

SADIE: Listen to me child…and you listen to me good. We don't take what ain't ours.

RO: But…

SADIE: We find a way out of no way…but we don't ever take.

RO: You're not listening…I swear I didn't steal no food. Wait I can prove it… It just showed up. I promise. Let me show you… Alright so I was standing here by the front door pacing, looking out the window,
(She stands by the broken window and begins pacing.)
And I thought to myself "Ro, I'm hungry". I kept looking out the window and I heard this voice saying "I'm hungry.", and I realized the little voice was me. That's when…

(There is a whisper of voices at the back door.)

RO: See I told you. Then when I go open the door, you just watch there is going to be…
(She opens the back door.)
Ta-da!!!
(…and finds nothing. She closes the door. She considers for a moment and…)
TA-DA!!!
(She opens the door again…no picnic basket.)
Okay, I know this might look bad but don't kick me out I swear I didn't steal from nobody. I swear it.

SADIE: I'm not kicking you out, child… You belong here. Just don't scare me like that by leaving like you did.

(SADIE lies down. RO shakes her head and goes back to the door.)

RO: Ta-da!!!

(RO opens it. A picnic basket waits for her.)

(End scene)

Scene 2:
Flowers

(Evening. Late evening…RO is attempting to scrub the walls from one point of the room to the other. She stops for a bit and she notices the ticket.)

(She picks up the ticket off the floor places it beside the picture. She picks up the picture and she sits cradling the teddy bear next to her.)

RO: *(Sings)*
Hey there compass, bring me home…
Hey there compass, I'm all alone…

(SADIE enters carrying a basket of rotten fruit, she turns and notices RO.)

RO: I couldn't sleep.

SADIE: Sorry to hear that, Angel.

RO: Just haven't been able to sleep.

SADIE: I know how that goes. I've had that problem all my life.
Never been able to sleep. Some things I guess never change.

RO: Until you die.

SADIE: I wonder sometimes if that's true.

RO: This weird thing happened, can't really explain it… Seemed like I was having a nightmare but I was wide awake.

SADIE: What did you see?
RO: I was standing in front of a mirror looking at myself…but the me in the mirror…she was different, She had her hair in ponytails and wore a white dress and long white socks and shoes. And she kept looking at me with strange sad eyes and she reached out to me.

Like I was suppose to take her hand. And I just… I just kept saying you're not me.
She just kept reaching and then she grew old and I hated her…I hated her for growing old and not being who I wanted her to be.

SADIE: I'm sorry about that.

(SADIE sees RO holding the ticket.)

SADIE: What are you doing?

RO: What?

SADIE: I said what are you doing?

RO: What?

(SADIE snatches the ticket.)

SADIE: Somethings are better left alone.

RO: Hey, look lady I'm…I'm sorry alright. I'm sorry…

(Silence)

SADIE: Ah, think nothing of it…shouldn't have snapped at you like I did. I have a present for you I don't know maybe you'll like it.

RO: A present?

SADIE: Yes, a present?

RO: I think I'm a little too old for presents.

SADIE: Oh no, child. Never too old for that…wait here?
(She exits.)

RO: She got me a present.

(SMILES enters the house…he looks around, he picks up the photo of CLARENCE, he pulls out a cigarette and lights it.)

SMILES: I love presents?

RO: What are you doing here?

SMILES: Hey lil' flower, I figured it out, you smell of lilacs… I like it…

(Pause)

Aren't you a little old for teddy bears, baby?

(RO puts the teddy bear down.)

RO: What are you doing here?

SMILES: Waiting.

RO: Yeah, well…I'm going to have to politely ask you to see your ass out.

SMILES: You want a smoke?

RO: No…and I'd like it very much if you didn't smoke in here?

SMILES: Make me…

(RO hesitates before she moves to SMILES and takes the cigarette out of his mouth and then steps on it.)

RO: There much better.

SMILES: Oh, lil' shorty got heart. How Mrs. Jenkins doing?

RO: I'd appreciate it if you leave, my momma is going to right back and—

SMILES: You ain't got to lie, angel, I know you ain't her daughter. Everybody in this neighborhood knows that.

RO: What do you want?

SMILES: Hey, girl…I just have a job to do that's all…and I intend to do it. Otherwise the streets will eat me alive. Let's talk, just me and you?

RO: What you want?

SMILES: You. Yeah, angel, I want you…

RO: You don't even know me…

SMILES: I knew you the instant I saw you. Looked at you and felt a change in my world… I saw you and knew you were different and I like it. I could smell your innocence from across the street.

RO: What makes you think I'm innocent?

(SMILES *approaches* RO.)

SMILES: I know cause I can smell it on you. Yeah I can smell it…I can smell it all over you, it's sweet, pure, beautiful. Smells like lilacs… That's how I know you not Mrs Jenkin's daughter. Hell, you not even from this place are you? You different.

RO: I'm no different from anybody else.

(SMILES *corners* RO. *Circles her hungrily*)

SMILES: No, no, no you different. Yeah… That tough girl act ain't foolin' me, lil' flower…you different… you different, you're a flower growing in a concrete jungle… People don't got that here.
They all got that nasty stench of pain and misery all over them. They sweat despair when they walk down these streets… They all smell of the gutter. Stinks so strong I got to twist my face up in to this…this *smile* just so the world don't realize I know the truth… That I know it's twisted secret. I know what all this is. The world don't want us to see but I know…this right here is hell and there ain't no heaven.
There ain't no heaven, not for us, not for me…not for you. Just hell waiting eagerly to swallow us whole. And then…then I see you…I smelled you. First time I saw you, lil' flower I wanted to take a deep breath of you… So that I know for just a second what innocence feels like.
Let me ask you something… You like where you are? Sleeping out here with some crazy old woman in a burned out shack? Sleepin' in the cold night air? Shivering? Dressed in… what's this, huh?

Nah, me and you both know you deserve better
than that. Look out across the street, over there. You
lookin'?

RO: Yeah, I'm lookin'.

SMILES: You see that place over there? The one with the
red door?

RO: Yeah.

SMILES: That's mine. I got a kitchen to cook in...pantry
full of food. Air conditioner you can turn on and off...
and a bed. Nice and soft, and warm. What you sleepin'
on, huh? Rags? Better yet... Where do you think that
delicious food that shows up at your door comes from?

RO: That was you?

SMILES: That was me...

RO: Why? Why would you do that?

SMILES: I just want to make you smile. Wouldn't you
like to smile every once in awhile.

RO: What do you get out of it?

SMILES: I ain't no saint, baby. Think of it as a business
transaction...I get what I want, you get what you
want...God bless America...

RO: And what's that?

Smiles comes up behind her.

SMILES: Your soul, I just want to inhale your soul...I
want to bathe in it. Take each of your soft sweet petals
spread them nice and wide and savor the very touch of
you. You get whatever you want in exchange. All for
the low, low price of your soul.

Smiles places his hands on her shoulder, he turns her
towards him.

RO: My soul?

SMILES: It's a harmless exchange...well kinda.

RO: And all you want is my soul and I'll get what I want?

(SMILES's *arms slowly pull* RO *into him.*)

SMILES: Maybe a little bit more...

SADIE: More of what?
(*She enters a basket of rotten food in her arms.*)

RO: Mama Jenkins.

SADIE: Is there a problem?

SMILES: Nah, no problem...I was just in the neighborhood smellin' the flowers, when I saw her over here. Figured I'd come by and say hi...I was just leavin'.

SADIE: I think that would be best.

SMILES: Before I leave? You mind if I speak with your mama dearest?

SADIE: Ro can you go wait outside?

RO: Again?

SADIE: Outside...I left your present out there.

RO: Ah now this is some bull—

SADIE: Outside child!

SMILES: I'll see you soon, flower.

(SMILES *brushing his hands along* RO's *cheek and she exits.*)

SADIE: What do you want?

SMILES: Did you think about what I told you?

SADIE: You don't have anything to offer me.

(SMILES *moves towards* SADIE, *picks up a piece of her rotten food and sniffs it...before placing it back into the basket with disgust.*)

SMILES: Oh, I think I do… Can't be satisfied eating this? Do you like food? Delicious food? Not like this…filth. I know you got to be tired of eating rotten fruit and old sandwiches found in dumpsters.

SADIE: How's that?

(SMILES *pulls out an apple, it's perfect in every way. He tosses it to* SADIE.)

SMILES: I brought you a present too. What a coincidence… No more rotten food.

(SADIE *looks hungrily at the apple.*)

SADIE: No more rotten food?

SMILES: All you got to do is think about our last conversation. Take an interest in the well-being of the neighborhood…the neighborhood will take an interest in yours… Bon appetit.

(*End scene*)

Scene 3:
Revelation 1:3

(*On the porch,* RO *stands looking outward towards the sky. She slowly takes off the hat and the doo rag, and then her coat, followed by her jersey with each item that she strips off she becomes more and more the image of a lost girl, very much alone and scared. She opens a box and pulls out a pretty white dress and white shoes. She puts it on. Lights fade out on her and come up on* SADIE. *She takes off her elegant funeral clothes and places on a long coat made from rags, it takes on an almost regal appearance.*)

(SADIE *reaches into her pocket and takes out the apple. She take a bite.*)

(*It's night-time.*)

(SADIE *enters the house and looks out the door to see if she's been followed at all.*)

(*The sound of a bell rings out. Once…twice…three times.*)

SADIE: Go away…

(SADIE *turns around to see* CLARENCE *reading a newspaper, dressed in all white.*)

CLARENCE: Says here we're on the edge of the Apocalypse. Can you believe that… Doomsday here we come… The battle between heaven and hell is about to begin. It's live in 3-D, H D T V, surround sound, all in black and white, and I feel sorry for the poor souls stuck to fend for themselves in the grey.

(*Pause. He looks* SADIE *up and down, he looks at her in perplex dismay at her apparel.*)

Woman what the hell you wearin'?

SADIE: Thought I told you I didn't want to see you no more.

CLARENCE: I knew you didn't mean that… Anyway, Sadie Baby, I would have been here sooner, it's been a crazy few days… Line must be a mile long at the registration gate. Been crazy lately, Tsunami hits in the middle of Wyoming, There's an earthquake that swallowed up Paris whole…

SADIE: France?

CLARENCE: No, Texas…and did I tell you that Yellowstone just blew straight to hell. And the road to purgatory just opened a little wider… We are indeed in the last days.

SADIE: Then why aren't you at work?

CLARENCE: They can wait, they ain't got nothing better to do. You said that girl's name was Ro La Branch?

SADIE: Yes, what's this about?

CLARENCE: I was on my way back and it hit me. Her name, her story should be written on the book. So I looked…cover to cover, backwards and forward, checked every inch. Wasn't no mention of nobody named Ro LaBranch.

SADIE: Well, maybe it's under her full name…I thought you said that you understood that I don't want you to come-

CLARENCE: Yeah, yeah, yeah… Listen I thought about that too. Looked through all them ghetto names, and do you know what I found? Nothing…

SADIE: So…

CLARENCE: So, something just ain't right so I headed right back over here. We got to go…

Clarence grabs her by the arm and tries to pull her through the door.

SADIE: Is this about concern for me? Or about you?

CLARENCE: Sadie, damn it why you makin' this difficult?
Things are about to happen here, and I'm telling you, now you don't want to be in the middle of this shit.

SADIE: I'm staying here with my house and I'm not leaving that girl. And what kind of language is that for an angel to be using?

CLARENCE: I'm entry level, woman. Who is this girl, Sadie?

SADIE: I told you…

CLARENCE: See I think you know more than you tellin' me.
Why you taking care of some lost girl? Have you looked at yourself lately Sadie Baby? Running the streets as a bag woman. Digging' in the trash and

sleeping in a burned out shack. You deserve a better life than that.

SADIE: You wouldn't understand.

CLARENCE: Well damn it, make me understand, woman. This isn't the life I planned for us.

SADIE: Yeah, well what kinda life was we suppose to have?

CLARENCE: Not like this…

SADIE: That's not good enough for me, Clarence…I deserve to know why you threw us all away?

CLARENCE: Thought I knew what happiness was… Thought I knew what it meant to be complete. Then one day I got to our mailbox and what do I find? An envelope that read foreclosure and I realized I ain't never had that experience of being complete. So what do I do, huh?
I kept finding myself looking at those bold red letters that said I had to leave my own home. The home I built with my bare hands. They told me that all of my sweat and tears and memories that I invested in this place trying to make it a home for me and you and our children was worthless. I looked at my hands dirty and worn down from doing long hard working all my life and…and felt them for the first time shake.
I couldn't take it! I felt the full weight of the world finally push down on me till I had to scream.

SADIE: I'm your wife Clarence. You could have told me. You should have told me.

CLARENCE: How could I tell you? How could I tell my angel, we was going to lose everything we had worked for. Right then, right there, I decided that I wasn't going to let them tell me nothin' no more…
No more of them telling me, I ain't got no more say in what I do in this life… To hell with them…to hell with

them all. I had the answers to all our problems. Fire Insurance, We still had that…
With that money, I could build you the home you said you wanted…the home you deserved. So what was there to gain? Everything. I couldn't light that match though.

SADIE: Clarence.

CLARENCE: I needed some courage. I loved this place too much to set it afire I felt myself dying inside as I poured that gasoline. So I bought me a bottle. Hell, I bought two-three bottles.

SADIE: Why you telling me this?

CLARENCE: You asked…I drank two of them and whatever was left I poured out to help the flame. When I set that house on fire that was the only time I truly felt alive.
That was me sending those bastards a notice that if they want my house then they'll pay for it. How was I suppose to know I was going to pass out before I could get to the damn door. So now you know. If I had known I end up losing you…

SADIE: Well you made your choice didn't you…left me alone, left your children shamed.

CLARENCE: You and them kids should be proud I stood up…

SADIE: You stood up?

CLARENCE: Yes, I stood up damnit. I needed to do this. Did I mess up, yes… But God recognized my sacrifice, God saw I was flawed and still found a way to forgive me and love me why can't you?

SADIE: Cause it was selfish…You think I couldn't see that you were flawed. I saw it but I also saw God inside of you and I loved you for both of those things. I would have stood by you, all you had to do is tell me… Now get out my house.

CLARENCE: It's my house, too.

SADIE: I said it once, I'll say it twice… Negro, your house burned down with you.

CLARENCE: Who you got living under this roof?

SADIE: Bye, Clarence

CLARENCE: DAMN IT, SADIE! Either stop this foolishness and come home with me, or tell me who's this girl!

SADIE: What business is it of yours? It don't concern you.

CLARENCE: I'm the book of Life, Sadie. It concerns me…

SADIE: Oh, please, Clarence just stop it! You're no book of life… Stop with the story-tellin', stop with the illusions. Do you know how many people are in this world? How much sin is in those people? That's a big old book. And I don't see nothing strapped to your back.

CLARENCE: Look at me!
(He rips off his shirt. Etched criss-crossed into his flesh countless hieroglyphs burned into flesh all across his body. He stands his arms outstretched wide, his palms upward toward heaven.)
As the walls to this house started to catch aflame, God looked down and tattooed on my body with fire the name of every soul that walks on this earth. Blue and white flames searing my flesh, but the flames aren't hot, they don't burn… they're cool and refreshing… Everything that weighed down on my soul melted like ice in that fire…
And as I stood in that fire I heard the mayor say to me that I was to be his new book keeper. He named me his

new book of life. All who journey in this life are etched onto every one of my pages… And you got some child, some girl living with you, under this roof, whose name ain't on the book. So yes, Sadie, it is my business. Who is she? Who is she damn it?!!

(SADIE steps back. CLARENCE looks towards her and pulls himself away momentarily collecting his cool.)

(CLARENCE reaches his hand out to her. She pulls away.)

SADIE: Don't touch me…this isn't about me no more is it?

CLARENCE: Sadie, I'll travel through heaven and hell to show I love you. I'll part the seven seas and tear down the sky for you. I'll do anything you want me to do, but don't ask me to let you go cause…I CAN'T.

SADIE: Don't…

CLARENCE: Give us a second chance.

(SADIE walks over to the photograph of CLARENCE and holds it close to her.)

SADIE: I love you Clarence, I always will, but I have to find my smile here in this world.
(She crumples the photo of CLARENCE and drops it to the floor.)

CLARENCE: All the glory in Nawlin' don't mean nothing if I don't got you with me to share it, Sadie Baby.
(Silence)

SADIE: You know, it seems like things are getting clearer to me… day by day… pictures… thoughts… memories… Me lying in a hospital bed. Our boys sitting around me.
(Pause)
I want to ask you something.

CLARENCE: What? Just name it.

SADIE: Where am I?

(Silence)

CLARENCE: This is Houston.

SADIE: No, no, it's not… Where am I really, Clarence?

(Silence)

CLARENCE: You already know don't you…say it… Go on and say it… Where are you Sadie May Jenkins, you tell me?

SADIE: Intersection between living and dead. Border of heaven and hell. But you couldn't tell me that, could you?

CLARENCE: You and that girl. Don't you see you're playing with something bigger than you. Baby, you're not suppose to be here. Says so on my book.

(SADIE reaches into her coat and pulls out the ticket and extends her hand out to hand it to CLARENCE.)

SADIE: No maybe not, but I am.

(CLARENCE backs away.)

SADIE: Clarence.

CLARENCE: I can't…
(He exits.)

(SADIE puts the ticket into her pocket and opens her pill bottle It's empty. She collapses into tears.)

SADIE: I just want it to stop, Lord.

(RO enters and sees SADIE. She moves slowly towards SADIE and kneels down next to her.)

RO: Mama Jenkins. Mama Jenkins, are you alright?

SADIE: I just want this pain that I feel inside of me to go away. I just want to know what it means to smile again, but I don't know what to do to find it.

(RO *strokes* SADIE's *hair.*)

RO: Ssssshhh.

SADIE: I just want my heart to stop hurtin'…

RO: Sssshhh…

(RO *lies down next to* SADIE.)

SADIE: I just want it to stop…

RO: Sssshhh…Don't do this to yourself.

SADIE: Go away?

(*Unsure of how to ease* SADIE's *pain,* RO *does the only thing she can think of and wraps her arms around her, and holds her tight.*)

RO: You can't just lay here like this.

SADIE: Leave me the hell alone, child…

RO: Mama Jenkins. You don't mean that?

SADIE: I don't want to look at you.

RO: Why? Did I… Did I do something wrong?

SADIE: You did everything wrong, child. You came into my life. That's what you did wrong.

RO: You just going to sit here and rot?

SADIE: It's better this way.

(RO *kneels down next to* SADIE.)

RO: My ass it is…

SADIE: I just want it all to stop. Just want the world to stop.

RO: You can't stop, Mama Jenkins. The world don't stop, so you can't… Besides what would the world be like without Mama Jenkins? You're the strongest woman I've ever know. You protected me when I had no one else to turn to, provided shelter, and you don't take shit from nobody.

Don't you know how beautiful that is? That strength that you have in side you, it's more beautiful than beautiful, It's…it's ummm…it's Mama Jenkin-i-ful.

SADIE: You trying to be funny?

(RO giggles…)

RO: Sorry…couldn't resist…I'm dead serious…I got no choice but to respect that. Head held high, remember you taught me that. Come on Mama Jenkins get up. I need you.

SADIE: What would I do without you?

RO: Well, I don't plan on you ever finding out, lady. Oh…I want you to have something.

SADIE: Me?

RO: Yeah, but you have to sit up if I give it to you.

SADIE: No, promises…

RO: Mama Jenkins? Come on…
(She moves to her backpack, takes the teddy bear and returns to SADIE.)
I want you to have this.

SADIE: I can't take this.

RO: No take it…I don't need it anymore, I got you. Just think of it as a reminder that I'm always with you. No matter what, I'm always with you.

(SADIE sits up and holds the teddy bear tight against her. With the other, she embraces RO and kisses her forehead.)

SADIE: And I'm always with you. Child…

(End scene)

Scene 4:
Crooked Smile

(Night time)

(RO enters into the house.)

RO: *(Sings)*
Hey there compass, bring me home…
Hey there compass, I'm all alone…
Once was lost…now I'm found…
(Pause)
Mama Jenkins…Mama Jenkins where are you?

(RO stops as she notices SMILES.)

SMILES: Hey lil' flower, you miss me?

RO: What you doing here?
(She runs out to the back door.)

SMILES: She's gone.

RO: Mama Jenkins?!!

SMILES: Why don't you sit down, Ro.

RO: Where's Mama Jenkins?

SMILES: Why don't you sit down.

RO: I'd rather stand.

SMILES: For me.

(RO warily sits.)

RO: What are you doing here?

SMILES: We should talk. You don't mind if we talk, do ya?

RO: Well, honestly…

SMILES: Good. We're friends right? So I feel like I can confide in you. You see I came to pluck my flower. Been looking forward all week to inhaling you and you know what? Once I'm done with you I'm going to pick away at your petals. Play a game of Love me not…

Ro moves to exit the house

RO: I think you should go. When Mama Jenkins gets back she'll make you real sorry.

SMILES: Who do you think invited me to come over?

(SMILES *inches closer to* RO. RO *takes a step back.*)

RO: She wouldn't do that?

SMILES: You sure about that?
(A long silence)
You poor lil' flower, You don't realize this but you're not suppose to survive here. Nothing beautiful grows here… Nothing but weeds grow here, nothing but weeds…

RO: Mama Jenkins!!!

SMILES: You didn't think some homeless woman is going to sit here and babysit you do you? Thought this story had a fairy tale ending… Well it does. She gave up on you… She told me so herself. Said she had her own burdens she didn't want yours as well.

RO: She said that?

SMILES: Wanted me to give you this.
(He picks up the teddy bear.)
Aren't you lil' old for teddy bears?

RO: I feel cold all of a sudden.

(SMILES *moves towards* RO, *he places his hand upon her shoulder.*)

SMILES: Come on over to my place…
(He moves his hand over her cheek, caressing it, then slides it down her arm and takes her hand.)
It's nice and warm over there.

(Pause)

RO: The house with the red door?

SMILES: That's the one…

(SMILES guides RO towards the door.)

SMILES: Bring your smile and come see me…

(SADIE enters.)

SADIE: Stop. Stop…

(SADIE rushes toward RO and SMILES.)

(She snatches, grabs and reaches trying to free RO, but SMILES bats her down.)

SMILES: *(He smiles.)* Did you enjoy the present, I gave you Mama Jenkins? Did you like that apple?

SADIE: Leave the child alone.
(She rises and moves to him again.)
Don't touch her.

SMILES: Stay where you are, old lady.

SADIE: Let her go, please.

SMILES: I've got what I've wanted now.

(SADIE marches forward. SMILES stretches his hand open and clenches it into an angry fist. She drops to her knees and gasps for breath, clutching her stomach.)

SMILES: Oh I got to tell you, I really hate doing this… okay maybe that's a lie… But see you forced me into a dilemma… You get these dilemmas in life and it really forces you to look inside yourself you know? It really asks you to step up your game. I mean souls that aren't suppose to be here show up on your watch, and you got to look inside yourself…
Really look inside yourself deep. You have to tell yourself Smiles, my friend, your good at what you do. As long as you've been doing this job you've been

good at it. Damn good at it… And not once has a single soul stepped out of line. Not once until some old lady and some silly lil' girl shows up and upset the balance of things… You have to tell yourself that if your going to keep this job, if you want to keep yourself from being swallowed whole you have to…you have no choice but to maintain the order of things. So what do you do? Let it go or crush it in your fist?

(SADIE *rises to her feet. Head held high*)

RO: Mama Jenkins no…please stay down…please…

SADIE: Head held high.

SMILES: Leave this matter alone and you won't get hurt any further old woman.

SADIE: I'm going to tell you one last time… Leave the girl.

SMILES: Or what?

(*He stretches his hand open and clenches it into an angry fist.*)

(SADIE *drops to her knees and gasps for breath, clutching her stomach.*)

SMILES: Where's your pills at now, huh?

(SMILES *leads* RO *closer to the door.* SADIE *rises to her feet. Head held high*)

SADIE: Take me instead. For the love of God, Take me and not that girl…

SMILES: Shut up!!!

RO: Mama Jenkins. Please stop your hurting her.

SADIE: Quiet, child.

(*Pause*)

Take me instead. Take what you want from me, but leave her alone. Don't harm that child.

(*Silence*)

(Slowly SADIE *moves towards* SMILES *and* RO.)

*(*SADIE *and* SMILES *looks at each other.)*

SMILES: You sure? The place I take you to...death is final.

SADIE: Maybe.

*(*SMILES *release* RO *from his grasp and motions for* SADIE *to step outside.)*

SMILES: Right this way then.
(He turns to RO.)
I'll come back for you later...

*(*SADIE *moves to exit and stops herself. She turns towards* RO *kisses her upon the forehead and strokes her hair.)*

*(*SADIE *pulls* RO *away from her and nods.)*

RO: Don't go...

SADIE: Remember death is never more powerful than love.

SMILES: Come on...let's play love me not...

*(*SMILES *leads* SADIE *out the door.)*

*(*RO *collapses to the floor and grasps tightly for her teddy bear.)*

SMILES: *(from off stage)*
She loves me...she loves me not.
She loves me...she loves me not.
She loves me...she loves me not.

(The writing on the wall flickers and fades. A violent light bathes the small house, then a pain-filled scream.)

RO: Mama Jenkins. Mama Jenkins...

(End scene)

Scene 5:
Lost but now I'm Found

(RO *sits rocking back and forth with her teddy bear.*)

RO: (*Sings, struggling*)
Hey there compass, bring me home…
Hey there compass, I'm all alone…
Once was lost… Once was lost…

(*When* RO *looks up and notices* CLARENCE *sitting looking at her.*)

CLARENCE: Where's Sadie?

(*Pause*)

RO: You're him. You're the man in the picture…

CLARENCE: You can see me?

(RO *nods.*)

CLARENCE: Where is my wife?

(RO *simply gestures outside.*)

CLARENCE: Pointing don't tell me nothing. Where is she?

RO: He took her… He took her…for my life. She…

CLARENCE: She what?

RO: She went out there with the smiling man, and he…

CLARENCE: Talk to me damnit…talk to me?
(*He rises from his seat and moves to the door.*)

RO: It was the strangest thing I ever seen. He led her outside and he pulled a flower from her mouth. It shone so bright…and he played love me nots with it and then when the last petal dropped and she gasped her last breath, She…she smiled. He dragged her body out there and nailed it to the red door. She's still hanging there. She's still hanging there.

(CLARENCE *moves out the door. Leaving* RO *alone momentarily.*)

(CLARENCE *enters holding only* SADIE's *robe of rags bundled.*)

CLARENCE: Only thing hanging from that door is these rags?
Where's her body?

RO: She was out there…

CLARENCE: Where is her body!!! Where is it!

RO: I don't know.

(Silence)

(CLARENCE *drops to all fours.*)

CLARENCE: I failed her.

(RO *moves towards* CLARENCE *hesistantly.*)

CLARENCE: I failed her again…I failed her again.

RO: Head held high, she taught me to walk with my head held high. You didn't fail her.

(RO *embraces* CLARENCE. *He pulls away from her. And turns to leave. He stops.*)

CLARENCE: What are you going to do kid?

RO: I don't know.

CLARENCE: Don't seem quite right to just leave you here.

SADIE: Then don't.

(The sound of a bell rings once…twice…three times…)

(The house shakes. The writing on the wall glows and pulses, the rags rises from the floor and take shape of human figure before collapsing once again to reveal SADIE *dressed in beautiful white robes.*)

RO: Now that's what I call one hell of an entrance.

SADIE: Watch your language young lady.

CLARENCE: I don't understand.

RO: Mama Jenkins?

SADIE: It's me darling.

RO: But he…I don't understand.

SADIE: The Mayor saw my sacrifice…
(She kneels besides RO *and presses her close.)*
Clarence, can you take her to the gates of the city.
She'll need someone to meet her there. She'll be alone
otherwise.

CLARENCE: What are you talking about?

SADIE: I want her to go with you.

CLARENCE: I can't do that. She's not in the book.

SADIE: Oh but she is…

CLARENCE: Sadie baby, She's not in the book, I've
looked.

SADIE: Am I in the book?

CLARENCE: Sadie…

SADIE: Is my name written on your book? Am I in the
book of life?

CLARENCE: You know it is, Sadie Baby.

SADIE: Then let her take my place.

CLARENCE: What?

SADIE: Look at her. Can't you see, the girl that I once
was.

CLARENCE: I don't understand.

SADIE: Look at her and see.

(Silence)

CLARENCE: See what Sadie?

SADIE: Clarence Elmore Jenkins sometimes I swear you are dense.

(*Silence*)

CLARENCE: She got have a ticket, for one… Not everybody gets a ticket…

(SADIE *pulls the ferry ticket for from her pocket. She offers it to* CLARENCE.)

SADIE: This will pay her way.

CLARENCE: But that's for you, Sadie…Sadie, our home…our life together… If you give her your ticket you're trapped here. You can never leave this place. Is that what you want?

SADIE: Do you love me?

CLARENCE: Yes I love you.

SADIE: Then take care of her for me, Clarence, has it really been so long you can't recognize the teenage girl that you once adore when we were young?

(*Silence*)

CLARENCE: What?

SADIE: Lord works in mysterious ways…
(*Pause*)
Ro…look at me darling… See this ticket. It's for you. It's first class ferry. One way for one person.

RO: I can't do that…

SADIE: I want you to have it. I want you to go to New Orleans, march in the parade in my place…

RO: What about you?

SADIE: Never been much for parades…I think you'd have a good time though. I even hear there's a house not far that you can live at. It's beautiful…all it needs is your love to fill the rooms. Besides, I'm where I am suppose to be. I realize that now. There will be other girls coming, other lost souls like you coming here soon. Someone has to be here for them. Try to take care of them guide them out of here to Nawlins'.

RO: What about him?

SADIE: He's a good man…and I'll miss him. But he'll take care of you.

RO: Mama Jenkins… Will you sing for me before I go?

SADIE: *(Sings)*
Hey there compass, bring me home…
Hey there compass, I'm all alone…
Once was lost…now I'm found…
Hey there compass, bring me home…

(SADIE kisses RO gently upon the forehead and releases her. CLARENCE takes RO by the hand and turns to leave. He stops.)

CLARENCE: I'll take care of her for you. I promise.

SADIE: I know.

CLARENCE: Looks like you get to keep the house after all.

SADIE: Looks like it.

CLARENCE: Sadie?

SADIE: Yes, Clarence?

CLARENCE: Sadie May Jenkins, you are indeed a saint, you know that?

(A swirling maelstrom of colors and lights fills the room. CLARENCE and RO fade away into the blinding light.)

SADIE: I know…

(Alone, she drops to her knees and scrubs the last part of the wall. She looks back and examines it. She pauses, notices the teddy bear on the floor and picks it up cuddling it adoringly.)
(Finally, she smiles.)

To all the souls seeking to find your way home, To those that are lost, seeking to be found. To all my lost girls, My name is Saint Sadie May Jenkins, and its my mission to find you and guide you home.

(As SADIE *smiles, the writing once again begins to glow and illuminate one by one till the beauty of it is blinding in its brilliance. The brightness envelopes her as she stands with her arms outstretched wide bathing in the light.)*

(End of play)

(Or is it?)

(A GIRL *dressed in a private school uniform, wanders alone she enters the house, she's frighten.* SMILES *enters behind her.)*

SMILES: Hi

GIRL: Who are you?

SMILES: Just a friendly face… You are beautiful…not as beautiful as the last girl, but you are certainly a treat to behold… Have you ever play love me not?

GIRL: Go away… Where the hell am I?

SMILES: Oh, you don't know? Well how about you let me show you…

GIRL: No-ooo…

(The GIRL *turns to flee but she's cut off by* SMILES.*)*

SMILES: Strange things have been happening here lately…
Girls like you just keep poppin' up in my neighborhood…
You wouldn't happen to know what's going on would you?
If there's a way in then that means there is a way out…

(The GIRL *tries to get away from* SMILES *but he grabs her wrist tightly…)*

GIRL: Owww!!!

(A flash of lights, the writing on the wall glows. And SADIE *emerges, she carries a long staff adorned with colorful rags.)*

SADIE: Smiles…

(Pause)

I'm gonna suggest you do your self a favor, let that child go, before I knock that smile off your face.

(Black out)

END OF PLAY

WHAT IS WRITTEN ON THE WALL

The words that have been scribed onto the walls were contributed by several women when asked during a recent survey, what single word defines a woman in all her essence these are the words listed below:

loving	crazy
fierce	insatiable
enigma	complex
vulnerable	body
force	classy
passion	earth
explosive	nurturing
regal	absurd
bountiful	strength
complex	unstoppable
beautiful	desirable
intelligent	nature
warrior	sister
nonsense	powerful
uncertain	delectable
mother	WOMAN

www.ingramcontent.com/pod-product-compliance
Lightning Source LLC
Chambersburg PA
CBHW052201090426
42741CB00010B/2359